The Essence of Complete Kriya Yoga Practice

In the Words of a Kriya Yoga Guru

Ryan Kurczak

Before practicing any meditation, yoga or breathing exercise outlined in this text, consult with your healthcare provider to make sure you are fit for such practices. The techniques and methods described in this work are meant for educational purposes only. The philosophy described is for your enjoyment.

DEDICATION

To my spiritual teacher and mentor
Roy Eugene Davis
(1931–2019)

To my spiritual friend and partner
Melissa Baker
(1976–2018)

Who taught me the real nature of
Love and Wisdom

~

CONTENTS

ACKNOWLEDGMENTS

This small text was made possible due to the support of our Kriya Yoga Apprenticeship students and the Journal of a Kriya Yoga Teacher Patreon community.

Very special thanks to the staff of Center for Spiritual Awareness, who has held the space for all the Kriya students over the years.

Special thanks to Mitch, Ebba, Donelle, and Shannon for their assistance on this project.

PREFACE

For nearly two decades, I was fortunate to have the support and guidance of an established and authentic Kriya Yoga teacher. During those years, I was able to attend numerous retreats with Mr. Davis. Often, we visited together in his office/chalet on the grounds at Center for Spiritual Awareness in Lakemont, Georgia. During weeklong retreats, I would sit in the audience and listen as attentively as I was able.

I was initiated and ordained to teach as a representative in the Kriya Yoga tradition by his own hands. His influence on my spiritual life, as well as that of countless others, was profound. It is because of him that the lineage of enlightenment continues for me and all the readers of this small book.

Roy Eugene Davis met Paramahansa Yogananda just before Christmas in the year 1949. He was accepted as a monastic in the Self-Realization Fellowship organization, was initiated into Kriya Yoga, and later ordained to teach Kriya Yoga by Paramahansa Yogananda. The honor, respect, and love Mr. Davis had for his teacher Paramahansa Yogananda was evident and clear.

Mr. Davis' experiences with Yogananda can be read about in his book *Paramahansa Yogananda As I Knew Him: Experiences and Reflections of a Disciple.* This book, like *Autobiography of a Yogi,* written by Paramahansa Yogananda, is an essential read.

I can remember sitting in the audience during many summer retreats at Center for Spiritual Awareness, listening to Mr. Davis speak about his experiences with his guru Paramahansa Yogananda. I remember hearing his own rich baritone voice share those stories which were later to be recorded in *Paramahansa Yogananda As I Knew Him.* Those are precious memories that help to anchor my mind in the infinite presence Mr. Davis always embodied.

I can remember all the times we sat together, drinking tea during private visits, when there were no official retreats in session. Mr. Davis would usually request that we join him at his office, or he would come to our guest house and sit with us in the living room. Nearly always, these visits were timed to begin before the sun rose. Then the hours would pass as the sun began to break through the trees, shining in the window, as we listened to his personal reflections on world events or more stories of experiences gathered through his long life.

No matter the content of the stories, we always found meaning appropriate to our own current life situations. It was as if he knew just the right stories to tell to help us along without the need to pry into any of our personal details. Always, it was a pleasure to sit with him. We came away from each visit with a sense of upliftment and clarity that assisted us in our daily spiritual practices and engagement with our life circumstances and vocation.

This little book is a transcribed collection of two interviews and one talk that I was able to record with Mr. Davis at Center for Spiritual

Awareness. The first section, *Conversation with a Direct Student of Paramahansa Yogananda*, and the third section, *How to Learn and Practice Kriya Yoga*, are two interviews I conducted one-on-one with Mr. Davis at his chalet. The middle section is a talk Mr. Davis gave to my first group of Kriya Yoga Apprenticeship students during their end-of-year retreat at Center for Spiritual Awareness in 2018.

Mr. Davis' words have been transcribed as accurately as possible. Some passages and phrases have been edited to allow ease of comprehension. For anyone who's ever compared the syntax of the spoken word with the prose of well-organized writing knows the two don't always align. However, Mr. Davis had a well-organized mind and speech pattern, so editorial liberties, while sometimes necessary, were few.

The essence and spirit of Mr. Davis' words capture the presence of what I remember it being like to be with him in person. (The audio and video of these talks can be found on the KriyaYogaOnline YouTube channel and also on *The Kriya Yoga Podcast*.) His words succinctly and simply describe what is required for success on the spiritual path. The purpose of this little book is to memorialize his guidance and serve as a written reference and reminder for what it means to fully engage the path of Kriya Yoga.

Of course, Mr. Davis has written many timeless works on the topic of meditation and, specifically, Kriya Yoga lifestyle and practice. In the pages of his own books, you will find more than you will ever need, spiritually speaking. Yet, over the years I have repeatedly replayed and listened to the interviews and talk transcribed here. The messages conveyed always served as a reminder and anchor for what seemed so obviously important.

Mr. Davis' presence and teaching style are directly reflected in this little book. The simplicity, immediacy, and directness shine through.

The final chapter in this small work is an excerpt from my book *Kriya Yoga: Continuing the Lineage of Enlightenment*. Useful med-itation techniques and guidelines for effective, simple meditation routines are shared in that chapter.

Many believe and promote the path of Kriya Yoga to be only a collection of meditation techniques and formulas that, if properly unlocked, will lead to immediate and permanent Self-realization. The Kriya techniques are profound tools in the process of Self-realization. Yet, it is the authentic embodiment and demonstration of spiritual ideals and revelations within our day-to-day life that open us to the full scope of what it means to be enlightened, awake.

It is my sincerest wish that you begin your Kriya Yoga path on a proper foundation. Combine the study and application of the wisdom Mr. Davis shared in these talks with a regular meditation routine, utilizing the provided techniques.

Through the words of Mr. Davis, recorded here, you will find the complete essence of what it means to practice Kriya Yoga. As a guru in the lineage of Kriya Yoga teachers, Mr. Davis shares with us a way to greater spiritual awareness. These words are a simple yet profound supplement to the spiritual practices of any and all who are devoted to waking up from this mortal dream.

1 CONVERSATION WITH A DIRECT STUDENT OF PARAMAHANSA YOGANANDA

RK: I'm here with the spiritual director and founder of Center for Spiritual Awareness. Roy Eugene Davis studied directly with Paramahansa Yogananda, and he's been my sole source of Kriya Yoga instruction and guidance for the past sixteen years.

Thank you for being with us today, Mr. Davis.

RD: It's a pleasure to be with you, Ryan.

RK: I've got some questions for you.

RD: All right.

RK: How were you introduced to Kriya Yoga?

RD: I, of course, was introduced, as many people have been over the years, by reading Paramahansa Yogananda's book *Autobiography of a Yogi* when I was eighteen years of age. Two years before that, I was fortunate to read two books that explained Raja Yoga philosophy. And so, I was intrigued by the possibility that here was a way to acquire Self-knowledge by one's personal endeavors and right endeavors.

And then, when I read Yogananda's book when I was eighteen, I resolved to go to California to meet him. (I grew up in Ohio.) And so, I did. That was in 1949. I met him two days before Christmas in 1949 and two days later had a private talk with him. He accepted me for training, and I was a member of the monastic community of Self-Realization Fellowship for four years after that. A little over two years after we met, he ordained me, and I was the minister for two years at a small Self-Realization center in Phoenix, Arizona.

So, that was my beginning.

RK: What were your experiences like typically with Paramahansa Yogananda when you'd spend time with him?

RD: Whenever I was with him, I felt a sense of omnipresence. I was aware of omnipresence and a deep inner strength, a spiritual power. Although outwardly his demeanor and relationship with people on a private basis was very quiet and very reserved, you could feel that presence of his consciousness. You'd just feel it.

I was with him only about two months at the Los Angeles SRF headquarters until he sent me over to Phoenix, Arizona to help out with the branch center there. But he told me to come back to see him every sixty days, which I did for the next two years (went back to California wherever he was and spent time with him). I would spend two or three days and see him privately then go back to Phoenix and continue my *sadhana* or my spiritual practice.

I was very intentional at that time. Being a monastic and living in a secluded environment, I devoted my energies and my attention to my spiritual practices. And for three years during that phase, I meditated every morning for four hours, from three to seven, and for about two hours in the evening. Mainly, because I wanted the experience of doing it and see how it was to do it. For me, it was very beneficial. My personality is such that I naturally tend to be introverted, so the monastic vocation was ideal for me.

After four years with Self-Realization Fellowship, after Yogananda's passing, I withdrew from the monastic vocation, and I was in the Army for two years in the Medical Corps. And then, in 1956, began traveling and lecturing and have been doing that ever since.

More recently, now that I'm eighty-five years old, physically, I've slowed down somewhat in my travels. But we still have our international outreach, and I still go to Europe every two years. And we have our publications and so on.

To go back a little bit, whenever I went to see Paramahansa Yogananda for those private visits, I never went with any pressing questions. I went for his *darshan*. You know the Sanskrit word *darshan* means to see and be seen by divinity. So, I went just to be in his presence. And I found, for me, that was the most beneficial experience that I could have (just to be with him and to absorb his consciousness and his energy). Of course, he always said worthwhile things. But then, I knew the philosophical principles already, and I was engaged in my spiritual practices. But just to be in his presence was an uplifting experience.

RK: I'm sure you could share quite a few stories, but you've got that covered in your book *Paramahansa Yogananda As I Knew Him*.

RD: Yes.

RK: Yogananda came from a tradition where it was important to have a continuing teacher-student relationship. However, some say that Yogananda is the last true Kriya teacher.

RD: That has confused many people. The lineage, of course, from guru to disciple goes on and has gone on for decades from Lahiri Mahasaya and Sri Yukteswar and the gurus prior to Yogananda. And many of the lineages of teachers that have gone on generation after generation are not involved with organization at all.

But when Yogananda passed in 1952, he didn't have anyone that he could appoint as his guru-successor at the head of the organization. He had privately initiated me and several other disciples and given us permission to teach and to initiate. So, through us, the tradition has continued to pass on.

But, Self-Realization Fellowship, not having a guru-figure in their organization but only a president and spiritual representative (and they have done very well), issued a policy statement and said that Paramahansa Yogananda was the last in the line of SRF gurus. Notice the wording: the last in the line of SRF gurus. In other words, the organization would not recognize any other guru or teacher at the head of the organization in the lineage of Yogananda but that his teachings would be the guru. Well, the teachings can't be the guru, as good as the teachings are. But, of course, the organization does have many men and women ministers who are well-trained to go out and lecture and to teach classes. So, the teaching goes on, but the guru-transmission from guru to disciple, teacher to disciple, continues privately and doesn't have to be related to an organization or corporate body.

RK: In your experience, the long years practicing Kriya Yoga, what would you say would be the most important quality a meditator can have to encourage full Self-realization?

RD: Well, there are probably several characteristics that are helpful. One is to be very intentional and to aspire to be fully awake and then to be willing to be disciplined in practice to stay with it. Many people, they start off with good intentions and high resolve, but they soon become distracted, or they become moody and so forth. Mainly, I think it's important to always have that ideal before us of being completely spiritually awake and not to think of it as an attainment or an accomplishment but an awakening to the realization of what we already are. And not to give up on that even during the occasions when it seems like we're not making progress but to go forward with the right positive attitude.

That's one thing that Paramahansa Yogananda advised for me over and over again. He used to say, "You have to go all the way (meaning you have to wake up completely in this incarnation), and you can do it." That's how he encouraged me. And, of course, I believed that from the very beginning.

Even before I met him, when I was in high school, I'd be reading books on world religions and different philosophical views. And when I read about the possibility of spiritual enlightenment, I thought, *Yes. I can respond to that. That sounds real to me. I can believe that to be true for me.* I had no problem having that aspiration and that conviction that it was possible.

I don't leave any room for feeble discussion about it takes incarnations to get there. And if you got bad karma, you can't make it. And if your astrological situation isn't ideal, you're doomed. I don't buy into that at all. All of the enlightened teachers I know have always said the possibility for awakening is any moment. It can be instantaneous. Of course, we emphasize the way of introspective meditation in the Kriya tradition, but there's always a possibility of instantaneous enlightenment even without introspective meditation. We can simply just wake up and just be there.

Kriya Yoga, as you know, is not a separate Yoga. There are the classical Yogas: Hatha Yoga, Bhakti Yoga, Karma Yoga, Raja Yoga and so forth. *Kriya* simply means action or process. And *yoga*, the precise definition is bringing together of attention and awareness with our essence of being. Sometimes, simplistically, you read definitions of yoga as union with God and so forth, but really the definition is very similar to that of the word *samadhi*, bringing together the attention and awareness with our essence of being. The result is realization, direct experience and knowledge of what we are. That is a culmination of right yogic practice.

Today, I'm sure you know, it's been estimated by polls that have been taken that there are probably thirty million people in America practicing some form of yoga. But most of them, ninety-nine percent probably, are practicing hatha yoga for physical benefit. This is all right. It's of value. But even the few yoga magazines that used to be somewhat worthwhile have all now become glamorized, and all the ads are on clothing and mats and cosmetics and so on. But behind the scenes (or this side of that), there is authentic yoga practice that can be learned and applied.

RK: So, basically, the idea is to cultivate the capacity to know that it is possible to exp-erience Self-realization and then follow up with the dedication to stick with the process until it's done.

RD: Right. And in the Kriya Yoga tradition, we say, as I mentioned earlier, that Self-realization is not an attainment or accomplishment but the processes, the practices: cultivation of compassion, disciplined behavior, disciplined thinking, meditation practice and so on. These weaken and remove what Patanjali called in his text, the *Yoga Sutras,* the afflictions or the conditions that inhibit our soul expression and interfere with our attempts to be Self-knowing. We weaken and get rid of these afflictions, and then we cultivate Self-realization.

This is simply the path of Kriya Yoga. It's very simple. Sometimes, we hear the term *Kriya Yoga*, and it sounds all very exotic. But it's nothing more than practical living, practical action of the right kind, which is basic to all enlightenment traditions and authentic religious traditions.

Patanjali defined Kriya Yoga in the second chapter of his treatise as austerity, Self-study, and surrender of the illusional sense of self in order to apprehend and realize the ultimate Reality. This is it. To remove the afflictions or the troublesome conditions and to cultivate *samadhi* or realization of the true nature, this is basically Kriya Yoga practice. Now, many people, after having read Yogananda's book, mistakenly think that Kriya Yoga is only a meditation technique because, in his book, he devoted a chapter to Kriya Yoga practice, and he emphasized the meditation technique. I frequently get emails from people from different parts of the world, asking if I will teach them Kriya Yoga. And when I point out what total practice, complete practice of Kriya Yoga is, they're sort of surprised because they think it's only a meditation technique (the *pranayama*, circulating the current through the chakras). But it's much more than that, obviously.

RK: When you've worked with a lot of people, and you've met probably hundreds of thousands of people, what do you find most often gets in the way of a person on the path?

RD: A couple of things. One is their tendency to remain identified with their small sense of self, their modified states of consciousness, and mind. They also have a tendency to be forgetful of their true nature and to forget, really, to think about their relationship with the infinite. In other words, they stay caught up in their little, small, provincial mental attitudes and states of consciousness, and they don't expand beyond that very easily. It's part of association with others who do the same thing and habit, I suppose.

But if we can get past and solve that problem of constant Self and God-forgetfulness (when I use the word *God,* I refer to an ultimate Reality not a personality) and cultivate Self-knowing (our awareness as being a unit of the pure essence of this ultimate Reality)— remember that that is true of us—that can be very helpful.

RK: A lot of people ask me questions about religion and Kriya Yoga (like overlaying different beliefs). Do you find that's useful at all or necessary?

RD: It can be useful for those who need religion, who need the structure and the rhythms of ritual practice perhaps. It can also be a barrier, too, or blockage because if a person's holding on to false ideas, false concepts about what God is, what ultimate Reality is, and what is necessary to be spiritually awake or liberated or have so-called salvation, if they're holding on to traditional, really wrong beliefs, this can be a limitation.

Delusions, the false beliefs, and illusions are two of the main modifying influences that interfere with Self-realization. So, if they're a good Catholic or a good Muslim or a good Buddhist, that is, if they practice according to the tradition and it helps them to be focused and calm and compassionate and to live right, it's all right. But it's not necessary to be religious to be a yogi and certainly not necessary to belong to a certain religious tradition.

RK: So, religion's more helpful just to keep you happy and functioning in the world well.

RD: Keep you happy and functional if you like to have a religious affiliation.

RK: Spending time here at CSA in the past, it seems to me you have a great respect for Ramana Maharshi and the idea of Self-inquiry. It seems that *vichara* is spoken of in the *Yoga Sutras*. Are Self-inquiry and Ramana Maharshi's ideas compatible with Kriya Yoga?

RD: Of course. Early on in the first section of the *Yoga Sutras*, there is brief reference to one way to Self-realization, through discriminative knowledge. You cut away everything that you are not to get to what you are.

In Ramana Maharshi's tradition, according to the publicity, they often emphasized Self-inquiry: "What am I?" He might have said, "Who am I?" but I like "What am I?" You are a what and not a who. But anyway, if we get down into "I'm not the personality. I'm not the characteristics of the personality. I'm not this small sense of self. I'm not what people think I am," eventually we get down to "I am the observer, the witness. I am changeless, pure consciousness." This is emphasized in Kriya Yoga practice by Kriya Yoga gurus who are reasonably alert.

I remember I was impressed by Ramana Maharshi when I first was exposed to him and the book by Paul Brunton, *A Search in Secret India*, which I read when I was in high school. I obtained it from the county library. Then in 1950 about the time I had read *Autobiography of a Yogi*, someone gave me a copy of *Life* magazine, and there was an article in there about Ramana Maharshi. This is about a few months before his passing. They had this full-page picture of him, a standard picture, where he's looking out with his beautiful eyes. And I remember still how impressed I was with this person, who was obviously a pure, saintly being because you could just see it in his countenance. So, I've always had great respect for Ramana Maharshi.

RK: A lot of people get involved in spirituality, and they start trying to dress the part or take on new names and these sorts of things. Is that useful, or does it help? What are your thoughts on that?

RD: I suppose it can be helpful to some, especially in the monastic community, if they want to change their name and choose a name that represents the ideal they're endeavoring to actualize or have actualized. If they want to wear under their garment a *japa mala* or a string of beads or an astrological bangle, it's all right, but it's not necessary.

We don't have to dramatically change our name and walk around acting super holy and pious in order to live effectively on the spiritual path because, really, it's an inner transformation, inner awakening process. Whatever we do outwardly that helps support our intention and aspiration, it's all right. But sometimes at gatherings, you see people dramatizing that they are on a spiritual path with the way they dress and the way they behave and the garments they wear, and it gets to be a little bit too much for me.

RK: So, if it's inspiring, sure. But if it's dramatic and drawing attention to yourself, maybe not.

RD: Right.

RK: Well, one final question I have for you today. Thinking about Kriya Yoga in the future, as it's moving forward through the centuries, what's your vision of Kriya Yoga? What's your vision of meditation into the future?

RD: Well, of course, meditation practice has become increasingly accepted world-wide. Today, as you know, there are millions of people practicing meditation who are not consciously on an enlightenment path, but they do it because they say, well, it makes them feel better. They function better. They concentrate more efficiently. Many business executives and so forth say it helps them to keep their sanity, to stay focused, manage stress. Some doctors recommend it for patients who are going to undergo a surgical procedure because it reduces stress and they heal faster after the procedure. Meditation is even now being taught at a lot of private schools for children as a short period of quiet time. They don't teach it with any religious overtone. But the Kriya Yoga practices that I represent, that I teach as a disciple of Paramahansa Yogananda, I think they're suitable for our times. And, therefore, we're going to see increasing interest and participation in them.

But, as you know, out of the hundreds of people, even thousands, who come to study in the application of the procedures, they either misapply them, don't apply them with diligence, or they get to a certain stage of peacefulness and tranquility, and they think they've got it all, and they stop there. So, this is always the big challenge for people who are endeavoring to be teachers or gurus or helpers. How do you keep people encouraged to stay alert and focused and on track so they can have the awakening experience they deserve to have? How do you do that?

You mentioned earlier that I have, over the years, interacted with many thousands of people all over the world. And, of course, many of them have passed on because many were older than me when I first met them many years ago. But out of the many thousands that I worked with in classes and initiated and so forth, only a small percentage have stayed with it. And even fewer among them really understand what's happening. But that's human nature. I do what I do as a karma yogi, and I do it as duty. And well, I like to see good results, positive results. If I don't see them immediately, I don't let it bother me. We have to love and care and do our best to help and provide assistance, but we can't let ourselves be traumatized if our right endeavors, as we see them, are not as productive as we would like to see them. We just play our role.

Some call it a higher power, but there's an evolutionary trend that is expressing through all of nature and in human consciousness. And I think it is responsible for the increasing interest in spirituality and eventually responsible for the enlightenment of souls. So, it will happen. I'm sure it's the destiny of every being, who is already, at the core, pure and serene and whole and perfect, to eventually wake up. And that awakening we call enlightenment. And with that awakening, we have knowledge, comprehension of the facts of life as life is. And that's how I see it.

RK: Is there anything you'd like to add before we finish for today?

RD: Can't think of anything. I think we've covered a lot of useful bases.

When I had my first interview with Paramahansa Yogananda on Christmas Day 1949, when he told me I could stay there at the headquarters and be one of his disciples, after telling me how to fit into the work routine and how often to meditate and what to read, he concluded by saying, "Read a little. Meditate more. Think of God all the time."

And the last verbal instruction he gave me two years and three months later just shortly before he passed. I was visiting him, and we spent about an hour or so together privately. And his final words on that occasion were these, "Don't allow your mind to be troubled by what others do or don't do. And don't look back. And don't look to the left or to the right.

Look straight ahead to the goal, and go all the way in this incarnation. And you can do it."

And that was his last advice. That's how he talked with me. When I was with him, he didn't discuss metaphysical theory and philosophical concepts or scripture of any kind or salvation theories and so forth. It was always, "You can wake up. You have the opportunity. Do it now." So, that's my advice.

RK: Thank you for being here with us today.

RD: Thank you for this opportunity.

RK: Take care.

RD: Would you like some tea?

RK: Yes, please.

2 ESSENCE OF COMPLETE KRIYA YOGA PRACTICE

15-Minute Kriya Yoga Meditation Session

Just sit upright and be as comfortable as you can be in your chair. Head up. And let your body relax. Put your attention up into the space between your eyebrows. And the reason for this is it helps to focus attention in the front parts of the brain, which are associated with concentration and creativity and impulse control and decisiveness. This region is referred to in yogic literature as the spiritual eye center, but you don't have to try to see anything there. But put your attention there. And doing that will also elevate your attention from subconscious influences, from mental activities, and certainly withdraw it from external conditions.

Put your awareness in the spine. Feel the length of your spine from the base of the skull down to the bottom of your spine.

Feel the base of your spine and mentally say Om. And imagine and feel a quickening, a vibration there at the base of the spine. Om.

And then, come up to the sacrum, the small of the back. Om.

The lumbar region in the spine, opposite the navel. Om. Feel it there.

Then up between the shoulder blades, the dorsal region. Om.

The neck, opposite the throat. Om.

Then up into the forehead. Om.

And higher brain. Om.

Now, observe your breathing, and let your breathing occur naturally. And for a minute or two, be aware of the air coming in through the entrance of the nostrils. Put your attention there so you feel the air coming in at the entrance of the nostrils. Naturally, there is a moisture there in the inner lining of the nostrils, so when you inhale evenly through both nostrils, you feel a cool sensation. And then, the air is warmed in your lungs, and when you exhale, it is warm. So, you feel that cool sensation at the entrance of the nostrils when you breathe in through both nostrils simultaneously and the warmth going out.

During the course of an average day, you breathe more than twenty-one thousand times, so breathing is effortless and natural. So, in the early stages of sitting to meditate, it can be helpful just to observe the breathing. And doing that helps to keep your attention removed from secular matters and from emotions and thoughts and memories and so on. It gives you something to be aware of in the moment.

And as you progress, then disregard the sensation of air coming in and out through the entrance of the nostrils and go up a little higher in the nasal passage up toward the sinuses and the forehead and feel air moving there as you inhale. This can also help you to be more aware in the front part of the brain or in the forehead between the eyebrows. Feeling the air flow in with a cool sensation in that upper chamber of the nasal passage. Then, after a while, you can disregard the sensation of air moving and just be aware of breathing. Again, with your attention focused up there in the front part of the brain, just let the breathing occur naturally.

And as you progress, notice that, as you become more relaxed, there will be occasions of temporary pause after inhalation and after exhalation (just momentary). And during those moments of pause, notice that streams of thoughts tend to stop and that you are in present-time awareness without the intrusion of thoughts. Don't try to suppress your thinking. Don't struggle with thoughts that arise. Just watch your breath. Watch your breathing, and during those occasions of temporary pause after inhalation and after exhalation, notice that you can be temporarily thought-free.

It's important to remember that the purpose of meditation is to calm the mind and emotions and to have attention removed from the changes that occur in mind and awareness. These changes are usually empowered or driven by impulses that arise from deeper levels of being that activate thoughts and moods. But when the mind becomes calm and even the impulses that activate mental activities are pacified or stilled, then your awareness can be clear. Then you can experience what is called superconsciousness, a state of clear awareness other than ordinary states, which are modified or conditioned with thoughts and fluctuations and movements and memories and so on.

The word *super* means above or beyond, superior to. So, it is sometimes referred to as the fourth state of consciousness other than unconsciousness, subconsciousness, and ordinary conscious awareness—a more transcendent state of awareness. Your awareness is very clear. There may be thoughts in the background, but they're not invasive or troublesome, and eventually even they settle down. So, the idea when experiencing the early stages of meditation is to observe breathing and then observe the settling of emotions and thoughts. And notice the clarity of awareness that naturally occurs.

Now, before concluding, turn your attention to the more than seven billion people on the planet. Radiate goodwill to everyone everywhere without exception. Wish for their highest good. Their highest good will include their total well-being, their health and happiness, harmonious relationships and environmental conditions, and above all, enhanced spiritual awareness. So, wish this for everyone. We do this compassionately with goodwill. And if you want to imagine the purity of your essence of being blending with the collective consciousness of the planet, that can be helpful in visualizing. Imagine the purity of your essence blending with the collective consciousness and beneficially influencing everyone and everything. So, as you do this, it is a reminder that your spiritual enlightenment is beneficial for everyone. Our consciousness is part of a collective or group or one consciousness, so when we are enlightened, then our enlightenment somehow makes the collective consciousness a little brighter, a little more pure, a little more clear.

Let's chant Om.

Om.

Peace.

The Essence of Complete Yoga Practice

This morning, I want to talk for a while about the direct way to nurture spiritual awa-kening. So-called spiritual growth is really an awakening process. And really, our improved understanding is the result of Self-revelation—an unveiling and coming forth, or at least a revealing, making available to us the knowledge that is already innate to us about our true nature and ultimate Reality and our relationship to it.

So, it's important to remember that we are, as spiritual beings, units of the pure essence of ultimate Reality. And, therefore, what is true of It must be true of us. And then, therefore, Its purity and wholeness and serenity and innate knowledge of Itself we must have within ourselves. And this is what Self-realization is all about.

The word *Self* is used with an uppercase *s* to indicate our essence, our true nature, our true Self-identity, in contrast to what Western psychologists refer to as ego or the small sense/confined sense of self-identity. The word *ego* is from German *das ich*, which means the I, the sense of I-ness. And unless we are Self-knowing, Self-realized, usually when we think of I, we think of this personality-oriented, mistaken sense of self-identity. "This is what I am."

But a little bit of reflection reveals intuitively and perhaps through intellectual discernment that we are the observer. We observe our thoughts and our emotions and our personality characteristics. And even this small sense of I exists. We observe that. So, we are other than what we observe. We are the witness, the observer, changeless being. And when this is consciously experienced, then we say it is realized. Before that, it is known about. And it's good to know about it. But when we experience it as being true, then this is realization. Realization is experience along with knowledge of something. So, Self-realization is experience along with knowledge of our true nature just as God-realization would be experience along with knowledge of that ultimate Reality as it is— not as we imagine it to be or formerly imagine it to be or what others say it is but as it is.

So, there is an ultimate Reality, one Reality, which exists. In Western culture, we refer to it as *God*. The word *God*, however, (not God but that which is called *God*) is only about two thousand years old. It was coined or originated by a man, a bishop, who translated the New Testament into old German dialect and came up with a word combined from German and Dutch that later was changed to the word *God*.

When we use the word *God*, we usually think of an ultimate Reality. But it's well to understand what that Reality is. It's not a person, but it has two aspects. One aspect is Absolute or pure and without characteristics or attributes. It just is. It is just pure existence, pure being. Has always been and always will be what it is. But there's an aspect of that Reality which has characteristics, energetic influences, and in Sanskrit, they are called *gunas* which mean threads. And these vibrations, really threads of vibrations, produce universes. So, there is an ultimate Reality. There is the pure, changeless existence without attributes or character istics, and there's the aspect with characteristics which makes possible manifestation of universes and their functions and operations.

So, we can know what that Reality is by direct experience. We can somewhat intellectually examine and perhaps get a handle on it—but not completely. And with intuition, we have more insight. But then when we experience it, then that is realization. But the first step is Self-realization, experience and knowledge of what we are as a unit of pure consciousness.

Earlier when we were meditating, I mentioned that the purpose of meditation is to calm the mind and the emotions and to clarify awareness so that what is true of us can be Self-evident or Self-revealed. It is apprehended and experienced. And we find this mentioned in Patanjali's *Yoga Sutras*, which is the basic text on Kriya Yoga practice, in the second sutra of the first chapter: *yoga-chitta-vritti-nirodha*. You don't have to learn Sanskrit, but it's well to remember that second sutra.

Yoga is really the result of the *nirodha* or the turning back and quieting of the *vrittis*, the fluctuations and movements in mind and awareness. *Chitta* is the field of awareness in which there is mind, sense of I-ness or ego-awareness, intellect, and ourselves as the observer. But when the waves of the mind or the wavelike movements in mind and awareness are stopped and we remain conscious, then our awareness is clear, and we have an opportunity to experience our true nature as it is.

So, the third sutra simply was written: "Then the seer, the observer, the experiencer abides in itself." That is, when you get the debris out of the way and the mind is clear and the emotions are settled and awareness is clear, there is only Self-awareness, Self-knowing, Self-experience.

And then the next sutra: "Otherwise, attention and awareness are inclined to again identify with external conditions." We've all experienced that. Perhaps we meditate, or we experience a degree of peacefulness and serenity. And then we come out of meditation, and before long we're involved again in our thoughts and our emotions and the stuff that's coming down around us and the news that we are exposed to through the media and so forth. And maybe then even become forgetful of our true nature. Perhaps we had a glimpse of it or a perception of it when we were meditating or at other times when we were still. But then, when our attention was directed outward, we forgot and became involved out there once again.

Of course, the idea is to get to the place where we are so Self-knowing, so Self-aware, so Self-realized that, even after meditation or when we're not contemplating higher realities, we are always intimately aware of what we are as an observer, as a being of pure consciousness. Even when we are relating to our small sense of self-identity and expressing through our senses and interacting with others and attending to our duties and fulfilling our purposes, inside we are always poised in Self-awareness, Self-knowing. That's the ideal, to get to that place . . . It's one thing to meditate to get to the stage what we call superconsciousness or transcendence where our attention is removed from mundane concerns and conditions, and we just abide in that awareness of being. And it's so pleasant and satisfying and fulfilling. That's one thing, and it's useful. But it's important to progress beyond that and get to the place where we are always inwardly aware of our true nature when we are not meditating.

So, we don't have to be reclusive or off in a monastery or hidden off in a cave someplace in the woods to be successful on our spiritual awakening path. But we have to understand that contemplation and inner peacefulness as a result of disconnecting for a while from external conditions is useful and beneficial, but we can't sit there forever in that internalized condition. We've got to come out and relate to the environment and fulfill our purposes in life. We want to be able to do that with full awareness of what we are and what we are about and why we do what we do and so on. That is possible. That is called the superior state of realization when you are always Self-knowing, Self-realized regardless of what you are doing (not just when you are internalized and your attention is pulled back and away from outside conditions that are possibly distracting).

Overcoming Obstacles to Self-Realization

What prevents our natural awakening to Self-realization? Well, obviously, one thing that prevents us, if we're not on that awakening path, is disinterest. Many people are just not interested in being spiritually awake. In fact, they don't even understand what you're talking about when you point in that direction. So, they're not interested. Even the people who are not interested in spiritual awakening and learning about higher realities eventually will be because their innate urge is to be awake. They may not be conscious of it yet, but eventually it will become influential. Another problem, barrier really, to spiritual awakening is not knowing what to do to nurture our spiritual awakening, not knowing how to go about it. Another barrier or obstacle is knowing what to do but not doing it. That's common, isn't it? "Oh, I know what I should do, but I don't always do it."

There are other conditions, too, that interfere even if we are rightly resolved and highly motivated and doing our best to eat right and think right and meditate right and do everything right as we know we should do, or at least think we should do. Still, there may be some problems that we have to confront and overcome.

So, in the second chapter of Patanjali's *Yoga Sutras*, Kriya Yoga practice is recommended. And it is first defined in the first sutra as (1) austerity or disciplined thinking and behavior or actions; (2) Self-study, which means Self-inquiry ("What am I?") using discrimination and meditation—discrimination to discern the difference between what we are and what we are not (that's helpful but also to meditate to have actual experience of our true nature); (3) rising above, seeing through this mistaken or so-called illusional sense of self-identity, waking up from this idea that we are this small unit of confined awareness and realizing what our relationship to a larger reality is. These procedures are referred to together as Kriya Yoga practice.

Now, the word *kriya* is Sanskrit, and it simply means action or procedure or process. And *yoga* in the *Yoga Sutras* is used as a synonym for *samadhi*, which is another Sanskrit word, and they both mean pretty much the same thing. The word *samadhi*, if you go to the prefix *sam*, means together. *Yoga* means unification. So, both *yoga* and *samadhi* refer to unification of attention and awareness with our essence of being, or Self-realization. Patanjali mentions in the *Yoga Sutras* these practices can result in Self-realization.

In the second sutra of the second chapter after defining Kriya Yoga practice, then Patanjali wrote, Kriya Yoga is practiced to remove what we translate into modern language as afflictions and for the cultivation of *samadhi* or oneness of Self-realization. And the afflictions are simply enumerated later on in that chapter. They could be psychological conflicts, could be anxiety, guilt, poor self-image, doubt, trauma of some kind, unwillingness to learn, inability to learn or to comprehend what is presented to one, addictions, attachments of various kinds. You know how it is with the human condition. There can be a variety of troublesome conditions that interfere with Self-awareness and clarity of awareness and happiness and freedom.

So, Kriya Yoga is practiced to remove them. That is, some of these conditions can be renounced or gotten rid of very quickly by seeing the futility of having them and the non-usefulness of having them. For instance, we can renounce guilt and regret and envy and jealousy and egotism, an inflated sense of self-importance. We can renounce all of that stuff by just seeing how foolish it is to hold on to it. No one is making us hold on to it. We're holding on to it ourselves. We choose to hold on to it.

So, you say, "Well, I don't want that anymore," and you just let it go. You don't have to struggle to overcome. You don't have to spend weeks and months in recovery in various therapies. All you have to do is just dump it. Get rid of it. You don't need it. Some will say, "Oh, well, that's just easier said than done." Well, that's because they don't want to do it. They just want to hold on to it for some reason or another.

A lot of the stuff that's troublesome, we can just let go of it. Just let it go. That's a positive step in the right direction. And if we have some habits that are debilitating, such as procrastination (not doing what we know we should do on time and in the right way), we can let that go. We can stop procrastinating. And if we tend to run ourselves down mentally or verbally with self-talk or verbal conversation and diminish ourselves and say, "I'm no good. I'm helpless. And I've made a lot of mistakes. And no one loves me. And God doesn't love me," and so forth, stop that talk. Stop that self/mental talk and certainly stop that audible talk. Don't ever say anything like that. You might say it once to your counselor or your mentor or your advisor to help you get your head straightened out. But after that, don't talk about that stuff. It's negative affirmation.

Negative affirmation is influential just as positive affirmation is. An affirmation is a declaration of something that is true or you consider to be true or you want to be true. So, if you affirm all these things about yourself that you don't want to be true, you're simply putting that more deeply into your subconscious. And it's a form of self-indulgence, self-punishment sometimes, and self-limitation. So, we don't need to do that.

There's a lot we can do to help ourselves live more efficiently and productively just by having the right intentions and following through. Patanjali mentioned in the *Yoga Sutra*s that progress in spiritual awakening is in relationship to the intensiveness of practice —not the intensity but the intensiveness or the concentrated right endeavor or focus. If we stay focused on what it is we intend to do and will do, just stay focused on that and go forward with that, then we can have satisfactory progress in awakening to Self-knowing or Self-realization.

In the *Yoga Sutras*, Patanjali mentions a variety of things that can be done (for people who want to meditate effectively) to concentrate and to clarify awareness. Contemplation of Om is recommended as a form of meditation. Patanjali wrote in the first chapter that there is this...we call it, in Western metaphysical terminology, the oversoul or the cosmic soul. Patanjali used the Sanskrit word *Ishvara,* meaning the ruler or regulator of the cosmos. Its existence is indicated, or really proven, by the fact that there is a vibration called Om. It's the vibration of the power of consciousness pervading the universe out of which the universes were manifested. But it has an origin. The existence of it indicates an origin. So, Patanjali says go and meditate on that and its significance: "What is this cosmic vibration, this cosmic sound that's everywhere present?" Well, it has an origin.

What is its origin? First, identify with that sound vibration, or imagine that you do, and then contemplate its significance/its origin and want to know it. And then that will get you to the stage of contemplation of the expressive aspect of ultimate Reality with characteristics. And go beyond that to the Absolute or the pure stage or aspect of ultimate Reality, which is experience of transcendence (what yogis call *kaivalya*, the Great Aloneness).

Now, some people, when they're first meditating and they hear about this as an aim or a possible experience or realization, get a little nervous: "Well, what if I experience transcendence and don't come back?" Well, that's not gonna happen. "But I want to be me." Well, again, that's the problem, isn't it? "I want to be the little me."

I saw it on the internet, I guess, someone had put a cartoon up that was taken from *The Wall Street Journal*, and it showed the caricature of the yogi on top of a small mountain—a reclusive yogi sitting there. And at his feet, there was a man who obviously had just climbed up the mountain. He still had his backpack on. And he was going to the wise yogi to get his input, and he said to him, "I don't want Absolute knowledge. I just want enough to get by."

Many people are like that when they meditate: "I don't want transcendental realization. I just want to be a little bit blissful. And a little more comfortable. And a little more peaceful." And that's all right. Be more peaceful. Be more comfortable. Experience a degree of blissfulness or joyousness. That's all right. But then, don't stop there. That's what yogis recommend, at least. Don't stop there. Aspire to go to the fullest extent possible, to wake up completely.

There can be those occasions of experience of transcendence. And when they occur, then you experience that they are very familiar. And they are not unsettling or frightening at all. But you feel like you're home. But you can't stay there forever because you come out of your transcendent state and back to ordinary awareness—hopefully, more illumined and more understanding and more functional. But if you calm the mind and emotions and clarify awareness, then there is the possibility of experiencing these transcendent states of consciousness.

And they can't be explained adequately with words because they are nonconceptual. You're talking about transcendence beyond characteristics and attributes. It's indefinable with concepts. So, you can hint at what it is, but you can't really fully describe it. In some of the Upanishads, some of the old writings from India, one approach to get to what it is is to negate everything that it is not: "It's not this. It's not this. It's not this. It's not this." Well, what's left is what is. But that's sort of a process of discernment.

Kriya Yoga, the term sounds rather exotic, but all it is is right thinking and right living and right contemplation of ultimate Reality, right contemplation of our true nature. So, if we don't use Sanskrit words, you use plain English, then it's just common sense. The procedures are suitable for everyone. That's why they're called universal procedures or principles. They don't belong to any religious tradition or any cultural situation. They're just universal.

Guidelines for Kriya Yoga Practice

The guidelines for practice are ethical living: truthfulness, honesty, harmlessness, freedom from greed or possessiveness, non-dissipation of your vital forces/right use of your vital forces and mental capacities, and then cultivation of inner calmness and peacefulness in all situations.

See, we don't have to be fully spiritually enlightened to live right. We know how to live. By now, you know, there's a lot of information about the usefulness of a wholesome diet, rest, exercise, positive mental attitude, meditation, wise management of resources. I mean, most of this is just common sense once you get a handle on it. So, we don't have to be spiritually enlightened to live right or to live constructively. All we have to do is learn how to do it and do it.

You say, "Well, I'm not spiritually enlightened yet." Well, that'll come along. But in the meantime, you're going to be living much more efficiently than you were. You're going to be healthier, happier, more successful in what you do and so on.

It's also well to know the aims of life that ought to be fulfilled so that we can be completely fulfilled. One, we ought to know what our purpose in life is. Our ultimate purpose is to be Self-realized. But while we're here, we also have things to do. We can examine our knowledge, our skills, what we have to work with, and how we can best apply that to living in the highest and best way. Not just getting by, but in the highest and best way, strive for excellence in performance of activities and in experience. That's called fulfilling our personal purpose in life according to our temperament and capacities and so forth. Two, we ought to be able to have all of our life-enhancing desires and needs easily fulfilled. Life should not be an endless struggle, putting up with challenge and difficulties, and just getting by, making do and so on. We should be able to produce and attract whatever it is we need or want to live productively, successfully, effectively. And once we can do that, then that's a big plus. And we should have adequate resources to enable us to be secure and free to express so that we don't have limitations. And then, three, we want to be Self-realized. I know some people say, "Gee, if I had the first two going for me, I might not want to be Self-realized." But you would because your innate urge to be spiritually awake would eventually become compelling.

One of my brother disciples whose picture's on the wall over there, James Lynn, he was Yogananda's successor as president of Self-Realization Fellowship for three years after Yogananda passed. He met Yogananda when Yogananda was lecturing in Kansas City in 1931 as I think it was. Mr. Lynn was born about the same year Yogananda was, about 1893 (within a year or so). When he met Yogananda, he would've been almost forty years of age. By that time, he already had two or three million dollars accumulated, and he was, in the eyes of others and himself, quite successful as a businessman/executive in Kansas City. He owned two insurance companies and was invested in other projects. But he said that, until he met Yogananda, hc was not completely happy, and he was nervous all the time—literally fidgety. But after he met Yogananda, he learned how to eat right and think right and practice yoga and meditate, and his life changed. The inner life changed.

He still continued to be very successful in business because he enjoyed business and he was good at it. But he was really a yogi, and he spent early morning hours and evening hours in deep meditation. And when he could get away from business in Kansas City, he went to California to one of the Self-Realization Fellowship retreats just north of San Diego. And he'd spend two or three weeks there, mostly in seclusion and going for walks and swimming in the ocean and meditating. And sometimes if Yogananda was in residence, they would meditate three, four, five, six hours together at a time.

He was a combination of what Yogananda referred to as "Western practicality and Eastern spirituality." Spirituality doesn't have to be confined to the East, but a lot of enlightenment traditions have had their origin in the so-called East only because culture was more developed there a long time ago before Europe and certainly in America.

We can live an active life, a purposeful life, and still be Self-realized. If you know what your purpose . . . why you are here, what you're here to do and get on with it, this is important to do. But set aside time for reflection. Set aside time for reading spiritual literature, learning about higher realities, philosophical ideas, how to meditate effectively. And then do it and apply what you learn. That's the important thing: to apply what we learn. To live it.

And thankfully, we don't have to be outwardly pious. No one has to know of our inward preoccupation with spirituality. In fact, it's better that way not to draw attention to ourselves and just quietly live our lives effectively and meditate deeply and exp- erience progressive spiritual awakening. And it will naturally occur in the course of time.

The important thing is to stay with it in the right way for the long haul. When we first start out, we learn about metaphysics and yoga and higher realities and healthy lifestyle. We may have this super enthusiasm, and we want to know everything there is to know right away, and we want to be highly realized in a few weeks and so forth. But it doesn't happen that way for most people. There may be occasions of instant enlight- enment, but for most people, it takes time. So, we have to settle in for the long haul. And when we're on the right track, resolve to stay with it faithfully and with confidence and without undue concern for the results.

I was, one time, visiting Master, Paramahansa Yogananda, at his desert retreat in Twentynine Palms, California where he went to live for the last three years of his earth life. He spent most of the time there. Occasionally, he went back to Los Angeles for special functions/special purposes, but mostly he was out there so he could complete his writing that he had outlined for himself. We were talking quietly one evening. This is just a few months after I had met him. So, I had this initial enthusiasm. And then, I wasn't depressed, but I'd gotten to the place where I realized, after six months, I wasn't going to be enlightened overnight and that I was going to have to hang in there. I didn't mention this to him, but he said to me, "Roy, you have to want God (that's how he put it; he means spiritual realization) with all your heart with such intensity that you can't wait another day to have that realization, but you have to be patient just in case it doesn't happen that day."

So, you have the intention and the intensiveness (rather than intensity) of focus and concentration and resolve. But you also have the inner calmness and emotional stability to wait and see what happens. You don't want to give up, but on the other hand, you don't want to become despondent. You want to stay even-minded, emotionally stable, and forward-looking.

In high school, I began to read books, which I borrowed from the county library, about world religions and read about Buddhism and other religious traditions. When I read about the idea of enlightenment, I thought, *Oh, I can be like that. I will be like that.* I didn't think, *Oh, wouldn't it be wonderful? But I couldn't do that.* No, I responded to it. I recognized it as a possibility. Consequently, all of my early life, I was highly resolved, and I purposefully did not talk about my spiritual aspirations with anyone. Even when I was at the Self-Realization Fellowship, I didn't talk with the other fellows about my spiritual aspirations. I didn't discuss my inner experiences.

And in fact, Yogananda sent me (about three, four, five, or six weeks after I met him) over to Arizona to help out with a branch SRF center, so I wasn't at headquarters. I went over to see him every two months wherever he was and spent time with him. But I didn't interact with the other fellow except to say hello. I never sat and talked with him. I never discussed philosophy. Never asked, "How were your meditations coming?" or discussed my inner condition. Never did.

So, one of the great blessings, I occasionally say this because it's true, one of the great blessings that Paramahansa Yogananda conferred on me was he sent me to Phoenix. There was one other fellow over there, senior minister, two years older than me, who was a good role model and quiet and paid attention to his duties. And we didn't hang around and talk. Here was a great blessing because I was like a Trappist monk. I had that private time all to myself. I had my duty, my work assignment, plenty of time to meditate, reflect, and be still.

For about four years, I had that secluded environment, and it was wonderful. I recommend that for everyone if they can fit it into their life schedule. It happened to me when I was eighteen to twenty-two. It was very useful for me at that stage of my life. It was very grounding.

See, I grew up on a farm in Ohio. You all know the story, I'm sure, so I won't bore you with it. Farm life was a good life. But, from my middle teens, I had this spiritual aspiration to be Self-realized and began to read widely. And then, when I was in tenth grade, I read two books in which the subject of yoga happened to be mentioned. (I didn't know that when I got them from the library.) When I read about yoga philosophy I thought, *Wow, this is a very practical approach. You don't have to believe anything. You just do it and see what happens.*

Then I read Yogananda's book when I was a senior in high school. I saw it advertised in a health magazine because I was into health and wellness and bodybuilding at that stage of my life. And in one of the health magazines, there was an ad for Yogananda's book, and I saw it and ordered it by mail. And when I read it, I thought, *This was my connection.* No doubt about it. I didn't have to be sold on it or talked into it. I knew that was my connection. So, later that year, I went to California, and I met Master, and he accepted me for discipleship training, and I entered into the program.

About a year later, we were out walking one time at his desert retreat site. See, the year before, I had rheumatic fever. Five months I was confined to bed. The next year, I was walking with him at the desert retreat and, just out of the blue, he said, "You almost died last year, but your love for God pulled you through." And then he said, "You have a new life now, and you must make the most of it. You came to me this time (meaning this incarnation) to help me with this work."

We had an intimate relationship in that he was very casual in making these comments. It was very interesting to be with him. He would just talk to you very intimately in this way. No big official pronouncement or anything. Just in casual conversation, he would say these things. But everything he said seemed to confirm what I already felt to be true. He was only confirming it. I didn't ask him for confirmation. But in the course of conversation, he would tell me things that let me know that he knew who I was and why I was there and what our relationship was and so forth. It was very revealing, really, and very satisfying to me to have that understanding relationship with him.

It got to the place, it didn't take long, that I was so in tune with his mind and cons-ciousness that I could anticipate what he was going to say. In conversation with a group of people, he'd be talking, and I could anticipate what he was going to say next (how he would answer a question and so forth because I was just sort of attuned to him). I knew how his mind worked and what his consciousness was like. And almost invariably when I visited him, before he dismissed me and sent me back to Phoenix, he would say, "You stay in tune with me because when you're in tune with me, I can help you. If you're not in tune, it's like having static in the mental radio, and it's more difficult to help you."

What he meant by attunement was mental and spiritual attunement, mutual respect and harmony. When you have that with someone, you know, you don't always have to verbally communicate. There's just that awareness of the other person's consciousness and being. It's like two people in one body or in one unit of consciousness. I had that experience when I was with him. Then I would be over in Arizona, three hundred and fifty miles from Los Angeles, and whenever I thought about it,

I felt like he was there with me. He wasn't there in his psychic body or anything like that, but I was aware of his consciousness or the consciousness that he experienced.

In the *Yoga Sutras*, this is mentioned also as a way to Self-realization, to identify with, emulate the mental attitudes and states of consciousness of enlightened people. If you know someone who is enlightened or if you don't know any person personally but you know about them, then imagine: How would it be to be like that? How do they look upon life? How do they see the larger reality? What is it like to be enlightened? You can sort of use your imagination.

You may not be able to imagine completely what it is to be enlightened, but you can imagine freedom. You can imagine being happy and free and unencumbered and competent. You can imagine that. By imagining in that way, you prepare your mind and your consciousness and your life to actually experience what you imagine. You become receptive to experiencing that which you imagine if it is possible to be experienced.

You see, the subconscious level of your mind doesn't know the difference between the memory that is the result of imagination and actual experience. It doesn't know the difference. Subconscious mind doesn't discern. It simply records impressions of perceptions. That's why athletes, for instance, and successful people in various endeavors frequently they will say, "Oh, I imagine myself succeeding. I see myself doing it." And by golly, they can follow through and do it. Or they see themselves having certain experiences or certain situations that would be ideal, and then they can follow through and produce those conditions. Or if they can't follow through/they don't know what to do, they hold on to the idea in their mind and believe that they are worthy of it, and pretty soon life conspires to provide it for them.

I'm sure you've all experienced that at times you've desired to have an experience or a thing or an object or to know something, and you didn't know how you were going to pull it off yourself. Then maybe you forgot about it for a while. Then, all of a sudden, there it is right in front of you. Life just says, "Here it is." You attracted it, or it was there anyway, but you didn't see it before. Well, sometimes, you can attract events. And I'm not recommending that we become sorcerers or manip-ulators or metaphysical magicians, but I'm sure you've all experienced from time to time events have occurred that you wished would happen, and they just happened.

I remember, oh, back in the '60s, for some reason, I wanted to know about the lives of some of the early metaphysical teachers in America. I was curious about Mary Baker Eddy, founder of Christian Science. And up until then, about everything published was authorized by the headquarters church in Boston, so it was all polished and glossy. It was only the image projected that they wanted to project. I wanted to know what kind of a person she was in real life. It turned out she was a very interesting person, neurotic and a mixture of conflicts and insights and executive abilities. A mixture of stuff. But I wanted to know the inner story, the behind-the-scenes stuff.

I heard that Samuel Clemens (he wrote under the pseudonym of Mark Twain), year before, wrote a book on Christian Science. And I thought, *Well, Mark Twain was an incisive person and an outspoken, critical person, and he would have dug up some interesting information.* And so, I thought, *Well, I should try to find that book.* I couldn't find it. It wasn't in print anywhere. Wasn't available any place I looked. But I thought, *Well, I'll attract it. It'll come into my hands sooner or later. And better sooner than later.*

A few weeks later, I happened to be in Dayton, Ohio to talk for the Religious Science church downtown. I stayed at a hotel near the church. One morning, I went out for a walk just to get some exercise, and I walked by this used bookstore. To this day, when I see a new bookstore I've never been in before, I usually pop in and see what's happening. So, I went into the store about ten o'clock in the morning. It had just opened. And the fella came out from the back room, and I asked him if he had that book by Mark Twain. He said, "No. Even if I did, as I recall, the last time it was published, it was one book in a matte set, so I couldn't sell you the individual book. I'd have to sell you the whole set. Just feel free to browse."

So, I looked around. And in about ten minutes, he came back in from the back room, and he said, "I just was opening some books this morning from an estate. I bought the books from the family of a deceased person, and I was just going through them. And there's only one book by Mark Twain, and it's his book on Christian Science." It was three dollars or so. So, I got it. I thought, *Well, the universe is very helpful.* I had to go to Dayton, Ohio, walk into a used bookstore, and have a fella dig it out of a box that had just arrived, but I got it. So, things like that can happen.

How to Cooperate with Universal Mind

We can be responsible for producing our own results, and I think we should use our executive abilities. But what we can't do ourselves, if it's worth having or doing, we can see ourselves having or doing, and the universe can be supportive of us. This is one of the basic teachings in the modern metaphysical movement here in America that started to blossom around middle 1800s. First, the influence emerged from the writings of Ralph Waldo Emerson and his colleagues, who also read the *Bhagavad Gita* and the Upanishads. (They didn't tell me that in high school. I found that out later.) That literature had just at that time recently been translated into English, and they got their hands on it and were attracted to it. Then, of course, there was Christian Science. And there was Unity School of Practical Christianity, founded by the Fillmores in the 1800s. Later in the early 1900s, Ernest Holmes established the Religious Science or Science of Mind movement. And, of course, then the yogis started coming to town. Vivekananda came in 1893. And then a few others came on the scene. Didn't make big public waves, but they were here. Yogananda came in 1920 and made a big impact.

The early New Thoughters are called Unity, Christian Science, and Science of Mind and so forth. They emphasized that there was one universal mind of which our minds are units and that we can interact with that one mind. Emerson, as I mentioned, having read the *Bhagavad Gita* and other literature from India, he wrote in one of his essays or referred to in his essays to the one mind common to us all. There was one universal mind or thinking principle. I have to sometimes define it because whenever I use the word *mind*, I'm reminded when I first went to Germany to lecture in the late 1970s. The woman who sponsored my talks there in several cities and traveled with me and the others and translated for me, she told me ahead of time that "Here in Germany, we don't have a word for *mind*. You say *mind*, but we don't know what you mean by *mind* when you use the word. So, please use the word *gemüt* or thinking principle." So, I said, "All right. I'll do that." Words are not always interchangeable from one language to another.

But we call it *mind*, that which thinks. *Man* is from the Sanskrit word *mana*, the thinker, that which thinks, thinking principle. That's where the word *man* comes from. We're not talking about the gender. We're talking about the species. But anyway, there's a cosmic thinking principle, or some call it cosmic subconsciousness. It's universal, everywhere present. And human minds and minds of critters are individualized units of it. That's the metaphysical theory. Therefore, our desires, our awareness of needs or wants, our imaginings, enter into this universal mind, which is inclined to be responsive to us.

That's why you can imagine your way to health, happiness, and success. Imagine yourself living the kind of life you ought to live and you want to live. Even if you can't get yourself into gear and do it with your will, you can imagine yourself doing it, and that is a big plus. See yourself doing it.

Athletes do that. Basketball players and golfers and baseball players and track stars and high jumpers, you know, often they will say, "Oh yeah, I see myself doing it, and my body just follows through." It's effortless when they're in the flow. When they're in the zone, they call it. It's just effortless. It just happens. So, use your imagination creatively.

Creative imagination is intentional, controlled. Uncontrolled imagination can be fantasy. There's time for a little bit of fantasy now and then if you're sort of daydreaming and speculating and thinking about possibilities. That's all right to fantasize a little bit: "How would it be if?" But you don't want to walk around in fantasy, in make-believe world all the time. That's not being healthy-minded.

And, of course, we don't want to believe what is not true. Many people in the realm of religion and philosophy and so forth, they have these beliefs that are not true, and they hold on to them. "Well, I was taught this when I was a kid." Or, "My family believes this way, and it's hard to get it out of my head," and so forth. People tell me that sometimes, you know. They say, "Well, I grew up in a fundamentalist church." Or, "I grew up in this religious influence, and I got these ideas in my head about what God is and what God wants of me. And I know better intellectually, but it's still there in the subconscious. And every time I start thinking about these things, these memories come up with these feelings and these moods associated with them, and it clouds my mind. It causes confusion. I think I know what to believe, but I find it difficult to believe," and so forth.

What is the Ultimate Reality of Self-Realization?

It's helpful, in my experience at least, to as soon as possible arrive at a clear under-standing or a rational understanding of what this ultimate Reality is. It is impersonal, and it is not a person. It is formless, and yet it is a Presence. And it is a Reality. It exists, and it is knowable.

But some people say, "Well no, I like my God to be a person (a big father idea, the Lord in heaven)." Some say, "Oh, I prefer a Divine Mother because mothers are nicer than fathers. They aren't quite as tough on you. They aren't as disciplined as fathers are." But God isn't a father, and God isn't a mother. And God doesn't have a will or druthers or desires. It's not that way at all. Try to understand that there is an ultimate Reality with these two aspects: Absolute or trans-cendent, and the aspect with characteristics which can produce and does produce universes. And then, see yourself, intellectually at least, maybe intuitively, as a unit of the pure essence of that ultimate Reality. Therefore, you are immortal. You are as immortal as It is. Timeless, changeless as

It is.

So, the ultimate experience, according to many mystics . . . Of course, yogis use language differently than some Christian mystics or mystics of other cultures, but they're all talking about pretty much the same thing when they're trying to describe enlightenment. In Sanskrit, the yogis refer to it as *sat-chit-ananda*. *Sat*, existence. *Chit*, consciousness. And *ananda* as joyousness of realization of being. So, it is conscious, joyous, eternal existence. We see the word *ananda* used a lot in yogic literature and defined as bliss. But it doesn't mean emotion. It means sheer exhilaration of realization of our essence. It's not just sitting there saying, "Oh, I feel so good." It's not that. It's a superior, more transcendent experience/realization.

So, it's useful not to settle in at any stage of meditative experience this side of transcendence. Master told me about this one time. He said, "Some saints are satisfied to enjoy the bliss of God-communion (the sense of communion with the larger Reality), and they don't aspire to go beyond that stage." Then he said, "But you have to go all the way." That means you have to wake up completely.

You can meditate and feel very peaceful. That's wonderful. Even blissful or joyous. That's useful. Or, you can have stages of extreme clarity of awareness, and that's useful. But the thing is, we don't want to settle at any of these places and say, "Now, I've got it. This is all I need. I'm there." And then, every time we sit, work to get into that state of blissfulness or joyousness or clarity of awareness up to a certain stage and then just hang out there. That is beneficial because it'll produce side benefits: a stronger immune system and slow your biological aging processes and provide you peace of mind and emotional stability. That's all useful, but it's not the ultimate realization.

So, whatever experience you have, it's useful to inquire: "Is there anything beyond this? Is there anything more?" And be open to the possibility of discovery. And eventually, you'll get to the stage where there isn't anything more, and you'll know this when you are there. You'll know it. But then you'll be fully awake, fully spiritually enlightened. Before that, you're not fully awake.

The idea is to be fully spiritually enlightened and to the stage what is called liberation of consciousness. And what this means is that your awareness, consciousness, doesn't have any dark spots or any delusions. No erroneous ideas or opinions. And no misperceptions. Whatever you observe, you perceive it with accuracy. Because if you observe without perceiving with accuracy, if you think you've got it when you haven't got it, then you have an illusion, a mistaken perception. And then, you may have an erroneous belief or an opinion.

To be liberated, to have a consciousness that's liberated, is to have a consciousness that's absolutely pure. And no delusions or flawed beliefs or opinions or misperceptions. Not even any troublesome subconscious influences. No residue from the past from memories or impulses that are still anchored in your subconscious that now and then become activated and cause you discontent or trouble of some kind or feeling of having been traumatized or abused or not appreciated or whatever. You don't have any of that anymore. It's all washed out. It's all gone. As they used to say when I was growing up in the fundamentalist church, "Your sins are washed whiter than snow." You're all cleaned up, and your consciousness is all cleaned up. And that's what it means to be enlightened, fully enlightened, illumined by the radiance of your being. That radiance doesn't come from the outside. It comes from within you because you are It. You are a unit of the supreme It or It-ness. So, therefore, everything is within you. That's a basic teaching, too, isn't it? It's all inside.

But look outside, have some confirmation or some input. But eventually, we realize It's all inside. That's why the awakening to Self-realization is really a process or processes of Self-revelation, a coming forth and an observation of that which was previously unknown. But It was there all the time. It was concealed. Not concealed by something that didn't want you to know but concealed because you weren't able to see It. But It's there. And then you realize what It is.

3 HOW TO LEARN AND PRACTICE KRIYA YOGA

RK: Welcome back everybody. I'm here again with Roy Eugene Davis, a direct disciple of Paramahansa Yogananda and also the spiritual director of Center for Spiritual Awareness, a Kriya Yoga meditation retreat center in Lakemont, Georgia.

Thanks for being here with me, Mr. Davis.

RD: I enjoy being with you always.

RK: I have some questions for you.

RD: All right.

RK: Many people ask me what is the best way to learn Kriya Yoga. So, from your perspective . . .

RD: The best way to learn Kriya Yoga, of course, is to have good source material. And it helps to have someone who is reliable, trustworthy, who has experience in the practice of Kriya Yoga to relate to.

First of all, maybe we should define what Kriya Yoga is. The word *kriya* is a Sanskrit word that simply means process or action or procedure. And *yoga*, in its pure definition, means the holding together of attention and awareness with one's pure essence of being or true Self, which is why we call that awareness Self-realization or experience and knowledge of our true nature. Kriya Yoga is not a separate yoga system. You know there are various yoga systems: Hatha Yoga, Bhakti Yoga, Karma Yoga, Jnana Yoga, Raja Yoga. But the Kriya Yoga tradition which I represent as a disciple of Paramahansa Yogananda uses the best procedures or methods of various systems of yoga. It's a matter of emphasis. Our emphasis is to have this aspiration to experience or realize the ultimate aim of practice, which is spiritual enlightenment.

Today, of course, as you know, millions of people are practicing various forms of yoga (mostly hatha yoga and yoga practice for health and psychological improvement). This has value. But in the process, I think, many times it is spoiled and commercialized. The full value of what yoga practice can offer is not completely explained.

Of course, hatha yoga and the other systems of yoga have their place, but I was always inspired, from the very beginning, to want to be spiritually enlightened. And when I was with my guru, Paramahansa Yogananda, he encouraged me to that end. His emphasis was always "You can be spiritually awake. And pay attention to the essentials. And get it accomplished in this lifetime." That was his major emphasis.

Now, I realize that the majority of people who are attracted to the practice of yoga don't have that strong resolve or high aspiration to be spiritually enlightened. They're not even conscious or knowledgeable about what spiritual enlightenment is. And many people, of course, like in the *Bhagavad Gita*, they start their practice of yoga because they just want some degree of physical improvement or psychological improvement in their life. They want to avoid or overcome some painful circumstances. Or some want psychic power or ability. But I think if the emphasis is to aspire to be Self-knowing and Self-realized and one will be patient and learn how to proceed and stay with the right practices that over a period of time (years in my experience), they will have satisfying results.

RK: So, how does one know that what they're learning is authentic? How do you know the Kriya Yoga that they're learning is an authentic practice?

RD: One test is to try it out. When we are aware of procedures that seem realistic and useful, to test them.

I remember Paramahansa Yogananda telling that in the early years, in the 1920s and '30s, when he travelled widely and lectured to big audiences in major cities of the country, now and then, a person would come to him and say, "Swami, I enjoy being with you, and I enjoy attending your classes, but how do I know what you say is of value to me?" And his answer was usually, "Well, you try it for six months, and then come back and tell me." So, you have to try it. You have to do it.

I recall another story about Yogananda. Someone was talking with him and asking questions: How do I know what God is? How do I know that it's possible to be Self-realized? How do I know it's possible to be aware of these higher realities? So and so says this. And this book says that. Master said, "You're like a person who's always talking about apples and the various species of apples and what others say about apples, but you haven't eaten an apple. And you're like that with God. Why don't you get busy and take a bite?" That's the key—to get involved in the practice.

So, I was very fortunate when I was seventeen and eighteen. I was first introduced to yoga philosophy by reading books, and I was attracted to the idea that if you do certain things, you'll have certain results. You didn't have to be a blind believer, but you could experiment. And then, when I met Paramahansa Yogananda, I had his example (he was a good role model) and his encouragement and his instruction. But he reminded me that I had to do a lot of the work for myself, that I had to be the one to examine my tendencies and drives and learn to live right and do right and to meditate and have the experience of meditating. So, that's what I did.

I was with him for a little over two years before he passed in the early 1950s. Then after that, I was two more years in the monastic environment. I was the minister of the Self-Realization Fellowship center in Phoenix, Arizona at that time right after he passed from 1952–53. I was there all by myself over in Phoenix. I went to California to attend functions at SRF headquarters like summer convocations and Christmas meditation and so on. But the rest of the time, I was there conducting Sunday services and doing a little counseling (not much). But most of the time, living very much as a Trappist monk although I was a yogi monk: up in the morning at four o'clock, meditating for four hours, attending to my work duties on the property during the day, again meditating for two or three hours in the early evening. That was my routine for two years. So, I learned by doing, and the experience was very beneficial.

RK: So, individuals who are not necessarily in a monastic environment, after they've been practicing for a year or so, how do you recommend that they live their life or approach the practice for the first few years to really get into it and make it stable?

RD: Not everyone can live or even is attracted to or adapted to the monastic life, but everyone can decide to be self-disciplined or disciplined to the extent of establishing their priorities. So, if they work and have a family or are married and have a family, whatever they're doing in secular life, they can still set aside time every day for inner examination and meditation practice and for a little bit of inspirational or informative reading (not too much). I don't recommend reading too widely diverse opinions and getting all confused but reading good basic information for inspiration and to acquire necessary knowledge. And then, put into practice what we learn. I think that's the important thing. All enlightenment traditions and most religious traditions teach the importance of ethical living and responsible living and growing to emotional maturity and cultivating, or at least having the aspiration to cultivate and have, a relationship with a larger Reality people call *God*.

Of course, you perhaps know, I'm sure you do, that the word *God* (not God but the word *God*) is only maybe fourteen/fifteen hundred years old since it was innovated because it comes from Dutch and old German languages. The word *God* is not used, of course, in the Old Testament or the New Testament, which was written in Greek, and certainly not in the Eastern scriptures. The first appearance of the word *God*, when it evolved from old German, was about in the year 400 when the first Christian Bible was translated into old German for the Gothic people.

So, whatever word we use for that ultimate Reality is all right and how we will think about it in the beginning. Many people, of course, are not able to conceptualize, imagine, or relate to an impersonal transcendent Reality, and so they think in terms of God as a person or having a personal interest in them or having wishes and desires and will for them and the world order. Sooner or later, we outgrow those ideas, or should outgrow them, in due time and begin to contemplate that ultimate Reality as it is, which has an Absolute or pure essence, which is trans-cendent, incomprehensible but realizable (incomprehensible to the mind because the mind has limits). And also, there is an expressive aspect of it with energetic characteristics, the Sanskrit word is *guna*, which make possible manifestation of universes.

This, in the last several years, has been my idea and awareness and increasing realization of what that ultimate Reality is. My experience is it becomes more clear and more real in the course of time. I've never had any dramatic enlightenment revelations. You know, sudden, dramatic conversion experiences. My experience over the years has been progressive clarity of awareness, more understanding, expansion of consciousness, more insight that has just sort of happened over the years. And, thankfully, is continuing.

RK: I remember you telling the story, one time, about how you asked Yogananda if many of the sages and saints in *Autobiography of a Yogi* were fully awake or enlightened, and he said, "Not many."

RD: Yes. When I met him in 1949 at Christmas time, I was only at the SRF headquarters three or four or five weeks, and then he sent me over to Phoenix, Arizona to help with the center there. But he said, "Come back to see me every two months." So, for the next two years, every two months, I took the bus from Phoenix to California and spent a few days wherever he was and had private time with him.

In the summer of 1950, he was living for the most part at his retreat house out in Twentynine Palms, California where he had chosen to live in order to have seclusion and freedom to write commentaries on the *Bhagavad Gita* and other scriptures. And I used to visit him there. I never went to him with a lot of pressing questions. I had access to philosophical information in books. I'd heard him speak publicly and privately to disciples, so I knew what he taught. But I went for his, Sanskrit word, *darshan*, which means perception of divinity. Just to be with him. Because when I was with him, just in his presence, I was uplifted. My consciousness was expanded. And he always said worthwhile things, of course. But the main thing was the attunement with his consciousness and what he was at the deepest level.

One time, I was over there visiting him, and we were walking around the perimeter of the retreat site. And he was quiet. We chatted for a while. I let him do most of the talking. I found that was most useful. He was quiet for a while, and then he asked, "Do you have any questions?" Well, one popped into my head. A few weeks before, I had been perusing his book *Autobiography of a Yogi*. And as you know, in the book, he told about how when he was a young man in the early 1900s in India, he would search out people who were supposed to be saintly (and some probably were) and examine them and sit with them and talk with them. And the thought had come to my mind: *I wonder how many of these saintly people by now are fully enlightened and liberated?* So, I asked him that question. And that's when he without hesitation rather nonchalantly said, "Oh, not many. Many saints are satisfied to experience the bliss of God-communion, and they don't aspire to go beyond that stage." Then he paused and said, "But you must go all the way." Meaning you must wake up completely.

He wasn't finding fault with people who liked to meditate to a stage of bliss or spiritual enjoyment or peace of mind or whatever pleases them. He was just saying that's not the end. That's only partial awakening. Of course, I realized there were not many of his disciples, that I knew at least, who had gotten to that stage of enlightenment or were even proficient in meditation practice. Not that they weren't good people. They were good people, good-hearted people, kind, compass- sionate, caring, devoted to their practices, but not all of them were successful in being fully awake before they passed. I don't have any judgment about that, but I observe. Mainly, because I was observing myself. *How am I doing?* Not in comparison to them.

So, I resolved when I began to read books on world religions when I was in high school. I got books from the county library. I'm still surprised, when I think about it, that little Warren, Ohio, a country town (mostly factory workers and small farmers), had books on yoga philosophy and world religions that I could borrow. When I read about Buddha and other saintly people who were said to be spiritually enlightened, my response was *Yes,*

I can be like that. I want to be like that.

When I was a teenager, I went to a fund-amentalist church with my parents because that's what you do in farm community. But I never bought into the doctrine that was being taught from the pulpit or in Sunday school. To me, it was not realistic. And it was only when I became exposed to so-called Eastern thought or enlightenment traditions which have their origins in the East that doors opened in my mind about the possibilities of Self-actualization—that is, bringing forth, eliciting my innate spiritual qualities. I always thought, *Well, if others have done it, I can do it. And I want to do it. And I will do it.* So, I've always had that aspiration and confidence that it's possible.

Then, of course, after I spent four years in a monastic setting, I felt that I had sufficient time in that vocation. And I withdrew from it and was in the Army two years and in the Medical Service after the Korean War, so I didn't have to serve in a battle zone. And then after that, in 1956, I began to travel and lecture and write and teach and learn by experience how to do it. So, I've been doing it now for the past almost sixty years, and I'm just as enthusiastic, just as interested in doing it now as I was when I started out. I realize from observation and experience that only a few out of the many people that I touch and have the opportunity of working with will actually get the message and be able to follow through and have profound in-depth results. But some will.

It's like Yogananda, when he used to lecture to these big crowds in the '20s and '30s (sometimes two thousand/three thousand at a time) in big auditoriums for eight or ten days and then follow up with classes that have a thousand or two thousand people, where he would teach them more intensively and initiate them into meditation practices. Someone asked him, one time, how many of those people have stayed with their practices. He said, "Not many. I knew that then that only a few would stay with it. But I was sowing seeds in the soil of their subconscious minds, hoping that some of them would sprout and do them some good in the future." So, we can only hope for the best for people, wish them well, and work as a karma yogi, really. We do our duty, and it's not a matter of ego drive/ego motivation. Our feelings aren't hurt if we don't get the response we would like to have, and we don't feel proud if we do see positive results. We just do our duty. It's what we do—and not attached to what we do or to the results of what we do.

I always felt, when I was a teenager, that I was called to the ministry. That's a term we use in Christian circles frequently, having a calling. But I felt, when I was a teenager, that I was called to minister, to teach. And I had no idea at that time what I would teach because I knew it wouldn't be the fund- amentalist Christian doctrine. It was only later, when I learned about yoga and then met Yogananda, that I had the opportunity to have more of an awakening and more of an understanding. And since then, things have just unfolded. Most of the positive, worth- while things that have happened in my life— although I have used my executive abilities and knowledge that I have been able to acquire to function effectively—most of the worthwhile things that have happened have just happened spontaneously. It's like grace: sometimes unexpected, unasked for, certainly unearned occurrences that are of benefit to me and to others. Things just happened.

Which to me is an indication that I'm on the right track, that life doesn't have to be a matter of constant endeavor/constant effort and hardship and difficulty and pain and suffering, that life can be enjoyable and satisfying and actions can be effective. It's just a matter of finding our right place and playing that role.

The Sanskrit term for that is *dharmic* living. *Dharma* has many shadings of meaning, depending upon the context in which it is used. Generally, it means rightness, right-eousness, the right order of things. It implies that which upholds, maintains. Whatever we do, whatever in our life upholds and main-tains us and the world order we could say is *dharmic*. It's righteous. If we're in our right place in the universe, doing what we are called or destined or best qualified to do, then that is said to be *dharmic* living. We are living properly.

The word *Hinduism* is a word that was coined or originated by foreign invaders many hun-dreds of years ago. Knowledgeable Indian people refer to what they teach and believe in their culture and spiritual practices as *sanatana dharma*, the eternal way of rightness or the eternal right way—often mistranslated simplistically as eternal religion, but it's not religion. The word *religion* is not even there. It's not in the vocabulary of Indians anyway. So, it's not the eternal religion. It's the eternal right way of living: right thinking, right behavior, right contemplation, right aspiration. Very much like the Buddhist precepts for living in the right way: right motivation, right thinking, right living, right practice, right contemplation. And the result is productive living. Hopefully, enlightened, Self-realized living or at least the capacity to be spiritually enlightened.

When I was eighteen, I'd read Yogananda's book *Autobiography of a Yogi*. Someone else at that time happened to give me a copy of *Life* magazine, published, I think, in May of that year. And there was a several-page photo-illustrated article telling the story of Ramana Maharshi in South India in Arunachala. And I remember there was a full-page photo of him looking straight out with his luminous eyes. And I thought, *Wow*. I experienced a *darshan* or an uplift or a blessing just looking at the picture because he was so obviously so serene, so peaceful, and satisfied with himself at a deeper level that just the picture was uplifting.

Of course, people used to visit him to just be with him and sit with him. He didn't always talk very much. Didn't give public lectures. But, now and then, people would ask him, "How can I be Self-realized?" And he would answer, "It's really very easy. All you have to do is be still."

But he was talking about that complete stillness of mind and emotions, a complete settling. Like in the second sutra of Patanjali's *Yoga Sutra* treatise where he explains the end result of yoga practice and that is the quieting of the changes and movements in the mind and awareness which allow the true nature to be Self-evident or Self-revealed, Self-shining.

He goes on in the following sutra or verse or aphorism to say, "Otherwise, attention and awareness are again inclined to identify with the influences that modify mind and awareness." That's human nature. People try to meditate, and common testimony or complaint sometimes is "I can't control the mind. I can't settle my emotions."

So, there is that understanding there that contents of the mind have to be quieted. Emotions have to be settled. Even the impulses that arise from the unconscious or subliminal levels from below the threshold of the conscious awareness. The impulses that arise that activate thoughts and emotions have to be pacified. And when that occurs, all that is left is awareness of being—if we don't go to sleep. The key is to stay awake. Don't go to sleep. Just be there in the moment. And all that remains is "I am the witness. I am the observer. I am the knower. I exist." That's it. There is nothing beyond that to actually experience or to realize. It sounds simple, talking about it, but obviously isn't that simple to experience because otherwise there'd be more enlightened people.

More and more are awakening in our era, our current time cycle. There are more people who are becoming at least interested in spirit uality. And more people are becoming intellectually competent. Of course, we still have a large percentage of people who are still too inward-directed, too egocentric, too self-serving, and confused and so on. But we look out on the world scene, we see a lot more people who are becoming responsible for taking care of the planet, taking care of each other, sharing their higher understanding. More and more people are practicing meditation today in all walks of life. Even many people who don't think of enlightenment or the end result of their practice meditate because they say, "I function better. I think more clearly. I'm happier. I'm healthier when I meditate on a regular schedule."

So, this is all to the good. I remember Paramahansa Yogananda telling me and a few other disciples in 1951 about his vision for the future of yoga in the West and in the world. He said, "In the future, yoga will be taught in schools. You will see it." Well, it's happening now. More and more people are being open to these ideas and to the possibilities of Self-discovery, and I think this is good.

RK: Over the many years that you've been practicing and teaching Kriya Yoga, is there any particular lesson or understanding that you've learned that seems most important to you from the whole practice?

RD: Main thing, I think, is once we are knowledgeable and we know how to proceed is that we proceed in the right way with right intentions and that we are persistent—but patiently so.

I remember one occasion I was visiting Paramahansa Yogananda at his desert retreat, and he was just talking quietly. And he said (he talked very simply), "Sometimes, we want to know God. We want to be Self-realized very quickly, and this is good. But we have to be patient just in case it doesn't happen the day that you want it to happen." He used to say, "Want it with all your heart. Want to know God with all your heart and expect to know it every day. But if it doesn't happen, don't give up." So, there's that balance of aspiration and yet patience.

Some people can have an instantaneous, dramatic, transformational conversion experience, a spiritual awakening that is authentic and enduring or the results of which are enduring. But most people awaken little by little. Even the people who say, "Gee, I don't see much evidence of progress." If they are living right and tending to their practices and every now and then look back (not to live in the past but just to look back and compare how they are now to how they used to be), they will see that they have improved. Also, if they read the literature (the *Bhagavad Gita*, *Yoga Sutras*, their favorite literature, whatever it might be, regarding spiritual matters) and if they notice that they are understanding it now more clearly and they are seeing something there they didn't see before, that's evidence of improvement.

I know a woman went to Yogananda one time, and she complained that she didn't have any dramatic meditation perceptions (no lights, no thrills up the spine, no ecstasy, no revelations, no contact with spiritual beings). And Master said:

Well, do you have more peace of mind?

Well, yes.

Are you more content inwardly?

Yes.

He went on and asked her a few more questions. He said, "Well, you're progressing then."

So, don't equate dramatic meditative perceptions with spirituality or spiritual awakening because many of the meditative perceptions that fascinate some people are mind-produced phenomena or the result of mental agitation or emotional unrest and not of any great value.

If we have pleasant meditation experiences, that's all right. But if we sit there and say, "I've got to feel bliss or joyousness," or "I have to see the spiritual eye," or "I have to get out of my body," or "I have to have astral vision and clairvoyance," these are time-wasting desires. And we don't need that. Sometimes, we can have unusual perceptions, but even then, they should be looked at with objectivity. No matter how profound our perceptions seem to be, it can be useful to inquire, "Well, is there anything beyond this? Is this the end, or is there something beyond this?" So that we don't get stuck at any level and think that, "Now, I've got it all. I have arrived. I'm the messiah now. I'm going to go out and change the world and share my revelations." That's a big trap right there. Just patiently persist in the right way with faith. That is, with conviction that the end result's going to be worthwhile.

RK: Speaking of getting stuck, after someone's been practicing five, ten, twenty years, do you have any insights on how to keep the practice alive so they don't get stuck in a rut or a routine and continue to grow and develop?

RD: Well, again, go back to what I just said. Keep inquiring: "Is there something beyond this that I should know? Is there something else I should do? Are there any troublesome conditions that I've overlooked that need to be overcome or let go or transcended?" Occasional self-evaluation can be helpful. That's all I know.

Also, think in terms of sharing whatever enlightenment we have in a constructive way with other people. We don't all have the mission or even the ability to teach, to write and so forth, but we do all have the ability to see for others their highest good and believe on their behalf that they can have it, that they can realize it. I recommend that every day (not only after meditation but whenever we think of the world scene or other people) that we just sort of bless the world with our consciousness and radiate goodwill and feel, perhaps imagine, that the purity of our essence is blending with the collective consciousness and somehow beneficially influencing everyone and everything.

The *Yoga Sutras of Patanjali* has advice for cultivating mental and emotional peacefulness and stability: to think in terms of having a friendly relationship with all people and all forms of life, be thankful for the good fortune that other people have, and to observe whatever happens in life with dispassionate objectivity—that means without undue emotional reaction. Just observe it. This way, we have peace of mind and emotional stability even before we are fully spiritually enlightened.

In the second chapter of the *Yoga Sutras* when Kriya Yoga is specifically discussed, Patanjali mentions Kriya Yoga practice as including constructive discipline of thinking and behavior, Self-inquiry ("What am I? What is my true nature?") using discriminative intelligence and meditative experience, and also letting go of this illusion or this mistaken sense of self-identity, the small confined sense of self-identity. He says this is what Kriya Yoga practice is, and it is practiced to remove what he calls the afflictions or the troublesome conditions in our psyche and also for the cultivation of *samadhi* or transcendent realization. So, we can remember what is the end result of right practice. But after meditation, we can sit for a few minutes and just see the highest good for everyone, which is their health, happiness, and most of all, spiritual awareness.

And then, whenever we think of someone or the world conditions are presented to us (as they are almost every day now on television), instead of becoming embittered and cynical and disappointed and fearful or depressed, we can say, "Well, beyond this is a higher possibility. Things are improving, and they will continue to improve." It's not a Pollyanna, superficial, childish attitude like, "Oh, everything is going to work out all right," and so forth. But actually seeing it in consciousness and having this compassion for everyone and all life so that we want the highest and best for everyone. Do our part to see that. And also, in our life, to help to demonstrate it or help to make it happen without being forceful.

I'm not for being an activist and taking to the streets with placards and banners. I don't think that's our way. Somewhat, I disapprove (with dispassionate objectivity) when I see thousands of people taking to the streets and shouting and displaying their anger and their emotion. I don't think that's the way to bring about useful change. Now and then, public demonstration has been necessary in the past like with Martin Luther King to break down segregation and so forth. Sometimes, people have to stand up, let their voice be heard. But most of the time, we can live quiet lives and not be exceptional in the eyes of others. Just appear to be quite normal but inside be different. I think that's important. The inside, I think, is important. How we are there.

RK: In this time, you've covered, I think, the essence of Kriya Yoga and the essence of how to practice well. I want to thank you for being here.

RD: You're welcome. It's always a pleasure to be with you.

RK: If you want to learn more about the retreat center here and Mr. Davis' work, it's www.csa-davis.org.

4 PRIMARY MEDITATION
TECHNIQUES AND ROUTINES

The following meditation practices, combined with the applied guidance shared by Mr. Davis in this book, are the first steps on the Kriya Yoga path.

Before undertaking the practices given during initiation, meditate using the basic procedures given below for at least six months. Once you are proficient in mantra, chanting through the chakras, inner light and sound contemplation, and sushumna breathing, you will be prepared to begin the specific Kriya techniques. Also, be sure to read this entire chapter before exploring the techniques described.

Basic Meditation Procedures

Meditation clears the mind of conditioning and elevates awareness above the influence of samskaras (mental impressions with the potential to influence experiences). Samskaras are like impurities in glass. The more impurities in our consciousness, the harder it is to understand the world and our relationship to it correctly. Kriya Yoga practice is concerned with understanding higher realities to the same degree that it is concerned with living effectively in our current incarnation. When meditation is practiced intelligently, we gain understanding of higher realities *and* can relate better to the situations around us. We know our spiritual growth is authentic when we are internally peaceful while also experiencing greater harmony and effectiveness in our day-to-day experiences.

When practiced with attention, the following meditation techniques are helpful in eliciting superconsciousness. These specific techniques can be used by anyone yet are considered to be valuable preliminary practices for those aspiring to learn the higher Kriya pranayamas given during initiation.

Beginning meditators are advised to sit for 20 minutes once or twice a day. Proficient meditators can sit for 45 minutes or longer as long as the practice is alert and attentive. Passive daydreaming, slipping into subconscious states, or sleeping are not useful.

Set aside the same time each day for meditation practice so that it becomes part of your regular routine. Dedicating a place in the house or a special chair for meditation practice is also useful. It may help to have a ritual, such as lighting a candle or saying a prayer.

Consistently practice the techniques until you can be superconscious. We know we are superconscious when we are no longer unduly disturbed by thoughts or distractions. We can sit quietly and calmly, yet alert and awake, when in a superconscious state.

Basic Mantra Meditation

Sitting up straight and comfortable, bring your awareness to your breathing. Take a deep breath and exhale, letting your body relax while keeping your head and neck erect. Then let the breath flow in and out naturally. Do not force the breathing. Simply observe it.

Once settled and focused on the breath, introduce the mantra *so hum*. Mentally chant the mantra. Hear the sound *so* resonating within your field of awareness on the inhale. Mentally listen to the sound *hum* resonating within your field of awareness on the exhale. To fully engage your attention in this process, imagine each syllable vibrating within your being.

Let your awareness be drawn further inward on each inhalation and exhalation. In time, thoughts and emotions will settle, and you will experience inner peace. When this occurs, ignore the mantra. Sit in the peace generated by practice. If thoughts, memories, or emotions emerge, repeat the technique to re-establish your inner poise.

Inner Light and Sound Contemplation

In Vedic teachings, Om is considered the primordial vibration that emanates from the source of creation. Meditate on Om to restore your awareness to its original pure wholeness. Om can be chanted audibly or mentally. It can also be contemplated by gazing into the spiritual eye and listening to subtle sound frequencies around the head.

In a quiet place with little external light, assume a meditation posture. Take a few deep breaths, relaxing your body on each exhale.

Once settled, bring your attention up to the higher brain centers. Be aware of the space between your eyebrows and the crown of the head.

With your eyes closed, gaze into the darkness of your closed eyelids. Imagine the darkness has depth and space. Lift your gaze slightly upward, as if looking at the top of a distant mountain. Continue to gaze off through the dark inner space of your closed eyes.

Now, listen for an inner sound current within your ear. It may sound like a high-pitched hum, a ringing, or another constant tone.

Examine this sound. Listen for any change in the sound. Listen behind the sound. Do you hear another sound behind it? Does the one you are listening to get louder? Continue to follow the sounds as they change and draw you deeper into meditation.

With practice, the electrical activity of the nervous system you are listening to will enable you to hear the Om vibration. Allow your small sense of self to dissolve into the sounds you perceive.

As you practice this technique, while keeping your attention in the higher brain centers and looking inward, you may also begin to see lights or geometrical patterns in your spiritual eye. When this occurs, let them attract your attention. Contemplating inner light may enable you to more easily hear the Om vibration. As you go deeper into the sound current, look through the inner light. Feel that you are piercing the light, as if you are moving through your forehead into the source of the light.

Just as the initial sounds you hear around your head are the electrical activity of the nervous system, initial light perceptions are the result of brain activity. To practice inner light and sound contemplation, you may want to practice the basic mantra technique first. The calmer and more internalized you are, the easier it will be.

Chanting through the Chakras

Sit upright in a meditation posture. Bring your attention to the base of your spine, your first chakra. Maintain your attention there for five to ten breaths. Bring your attention up to the second chakra. Rest there for a few moments.

Continue bringing your attention up through the chakras to the crown chakra. As you go up through the chakras, mentally chant the appropriate mantra at each chakra.

Chakra	Location	Mantric Syllable
Root	Base of the spine	Lum
Sacrum	Small of the back	Vum
Navel	Behind the navel	Rum
Heart	Between the shoulder blades	Yum
Throat	Back of the neck	Hum
Third Eye	Between the eyebrows	Om
Crown	Higher brain	Bum

Then go down to the base of your spine, chanting the mantra at each chakra. Repeat the procedure two or three times. Conclude your practice at the crown chakra.

Sushumna Breathing

To practice sushumna breathing, meditate as you normally do. When the mind is calm and emotions settled, put your attention in your spine. Feel your spine from the base to the crown chakra. Imagine a hollow tube within the spine.

Breathe slightly deeper than normal and in a relaxed manner. As you inhale, use a gentle act of will to pull your life force up through the hollow tube in your spine. If you do not feel a sensation of prana ascending through the spine, imagine what it would feel like. When the inhalation is complete, the pranic current will be in the crown chakra. Hold your breath for a second, and then exhale easily and without force while noting the descending flow of the current. Let the breath exhale of its own accord. Do not force the breath out. Let the energetic current flow back down your spine like water.

When silence prevails in your awareness and you are absorbed in existence-being, pull the current up to the top of the head one last time. Let your breathing occur naturally.

Keep the current and your attention in the crown chakra. Sit in the silence until you conclude your meditation practice.

The Basic Pattern of Meditation

Over the years, as my capacity to meditate deepened and lengthened, I have followed one basic pattern. I have not deviated from this pattern since I began practicing meditation. I have taken note of this pattern and shared it repeatedly because I have noticed that one of the major obstacles most meditators seem to have is the inability to structure an effective meditation session based on their current skill level.

Step 1: Before entering my sacred space, I decide which meditation techniques I will be utilizing today. This way, I won't have to wonder about it. I know the process I intend to do before I begin.

Step 2: I enter the sacred space and sit comfortably and upright. I take a moment to become aware of my surroundings. I pay attention to all the input coming into my senses. I pay attention to how I feel in my body and mind. I just observe and acknowledge.

Step 3: If I have a ritual, such as lighting incense or a candle or gazing at images of people or divinities I consider enlightened, I do so.

Step 4: I take an easy, deep breath, exhale, and relax. I close my eyes and turn my attention within.

Step 5: I acknowledge the innate divinity within and around me. I acknowledge the innate divine nature of all people, places and things. (If you are attached to a guru, it can be a good time to acknowledge that person's positive connection in your life.) I feel as though I am not a limited personality but feel that I am infinite consciousness and that every breath, moment, thought, feeling and experience is an expression of the wholeness of life.

Step 6: I begin my chosen meditation technique, typically chanting through the chakras, sushumna breathing or mantra. I will continue this technique either until I have completed the set number of repetitions or until I feel my consciousness serene and internalized.

Step 7: I will sit quietly with my attention in the higher brain centers for as long as the internalized serenity lasts. I simply sit, watch, and observe.

Step 8: I repeat Steps 6 and 7 two or three more times. This depends on how many techniques I have decided to practice.

Step 9: I once again imagine all of consciousness as an expression of one whole infinite seamless being. I imagine and see all the people, places, things, and situations in my life imbued with the sense of serenity, peace, and Self-knowledge. I then expand awareness to include all beings in all times in every realm. I see them as an expression of my very Self. I see them imbued with that same sense of love, fulfillment, and Self-knowledge.

Step 10: When I feel ready (or my timer goes off), I open my eyes and go about my day.

For more information on meditation techniques and routines for intermediate and advanced practice, please see chapter 6 in the book *Kriya Yoga Vichara*.

VIDEO RECORDINGS AND AUDIO OF THESE TALKS ARE AVAILABLE AT:

The Kriya Yoga Podcast

(Audio)

A Conversation with a Direct Student of Paramahansa Yogananda – Episode 26 – Released August 24th, 2020.

The Essence of Complete Kriya Yoga Meditation Practice – Episode 28 – Released September 21st, 2020.

Kriya Yoga In the Words of Roy Eugene Davis – Episode 30 – Released October 19th, 2020.

The KriyaYogaOnline Youtube Channel

(Audio and Video)

Conversation with Kriya Yoga Teacher and Direct Student of Paramahansa Yogananda – Released September 14th, 2016

How to Learn Kriya Yoga, How to Practice Kriya Yoga, with a Direct Student of Yogananda – Released November 26th, 2017.

It is well worth the time to listen to Mr. Davis' own voice share this information through these recordings.

BOOKS BY THE AUTHOR

Spirituality

A Course in Tranquility

Kriya Yoga: Continuing the Lineage of Enlightenment
(Includes a full commentary on the

Yoga Sutras of Patanjali)

Kriya Yoga Vichara

Mahavatar Babaji and the Garden of Faith

Astrology

The Art and Science of Vedic Astrology
Volume 1

The Art and Science of Vedic Astrology
Volume 2

ABOUT THE AUTHOR

Ryan Kurczak is a meditation teacher, writer, and director of the two-year Kriya Yoga Apprenticeship Program offered through www.KriyaYogaOnline.com.

Ryan was ordained by Roy Eugene Davis, a direct student of Paramahansa Yogananda, and authorized to teach Kriya Yoga in 2005. He has taught yoga philosophy and meditation practices at retreat centers, Unity churches, yoga centers, and for various yoga teacher training programs internationally.

He is the host of *The Kriya Yoga Podcast* and the KriyaYogaOnline YouTube channel. For many years, he served as a Vedic astrologer and teacher of astrology.

Ryan Kurczak is the author of several books on spiritual practice and Vedic astrology.

Made in the USA
Middletown, DE
29 May 2023

31294739R00071